ABOUT GLASS

M000249033

People all over the world enjoy making things with glass beads.

Let's learn the basics before starting.

KINDS OF BEADS

The tiny beads used for these miniatures can be purchased in packets at handicraft, stationery of hobby shops. They come in various shapes. Most common are circular beads and spaghetti-shaped ones, called bugle beads in the United States. Circular beads come in verious sizes: small, large, and extra large, with the 2.2mm and 3mm sizes used most frequently. Bugle beads are 1.5mm, 3mm, 6mm, 9mm, with the 3 mm and 6mm sizes the most useful.

Other shapes include curved beads, pearl beads, ovals, and hexagonals. Spangle, rhinestone, and acrylic-mirror beads make occasional appearance too.

WHAT TO BUY
Beads which come threaded are called threaded beads.
Loose beads come in small cellophane packets. Loose beads are more convenient for making miniatures.

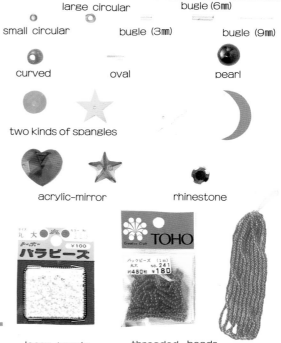

small circular • large circular • bugle (6mm) • bugle (3mm) • bugle (9mm)
curved • oval • pearl
two kinds of spangles
acrylic-mirror • rhinestone
loose beads • threaded beads

BEADING WIRE, THREAD, NEEDLES, NYLON FILAMENT

Beading wire and nylon craft filament are easy to handle and convenient.

BEADING WIRE
The wire used to make miniatures and accessories is sold at hobby shops in small spools according to thickness, either 28, 30, or 34 gauge. Flowers or leaves can be made by bending beaded wire into desired shapes. Be careful not to twist or bend the wire too hard of it will snap. Straighten twisted wire carefully

CRAFT FILAMENT
Nylon filament is often used in making accessories such as necklaces or rings Where flexibility is desired rather than rigid construction.

BEADING THREAD
Thread is used in the same way as filament. Polyester beading thread is strong and easy to handle.

CUTTING WIRE, FILAMENT AND THREAD
Allow for 10-15cm (4-6") more than you need to make a miniature. The extra length is easier to work with and can be used to attach beads to hairpins or other objects. The measurements indicated in this book include the extra lengths.

If the wire breaks while you are working, or if you decide it is too short, tie an extra length where the knot won't show and continue threading the beads.

BEADING NEEDLES
Beading needles are finer and longer than ordinary needles and are sold at hobby shops. Some packets of needles come with a convenient threader. These needles are also used for bead embroidery.

HOW TO MOVE BEADS

HOW TO HANDLE THREADED BEADS

If you cut the thread of strung beads, the beads will come apart. To avoid this, follow the illustration.

Untie knot

Pass end of thread through a bead and tie with a half hitch.

HOW TO MOVE BEADS TO ANOTHER THREAD

Fold the new thread in two and tie to end of the strung beads.

Tie

new thread

Move beads with fingertip.

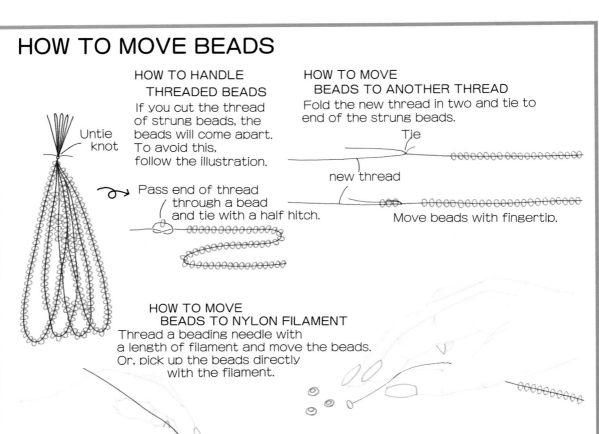

HOW TO MOVE BEADS TO NYLON FILAMENT

Thread a beading needle with a length of filament and move the beads. Or, pick up the beads directly with the filament.

Stretch thread tightly

wire

cellophane tape

HOW TO MOVE THREADED BEADS TO WIRE

Draw the end of the wire through your hands and lay it straight on the table, secured by cellophane tape. Push the wire through the beads.

ENDINGS

WIRE

After finishing work, twist wires tightly and pass through beads.

Twist wires.   Pass through beads.

Twist wires around two or three rows.

NYLON FILAMENT, THREAD

Tie a tight knot and repeat a few times. Then cut filament or thread. Put a little glue on knot.

knot

Pass through a special bead celled "beed tip with hole"and a small circular bead. Tie a tight knot and repeat a few times. Put a little glue on it.

RUNNING OUT OF WIRE

Bring to an end the wire you have been using, and start again with a new one.

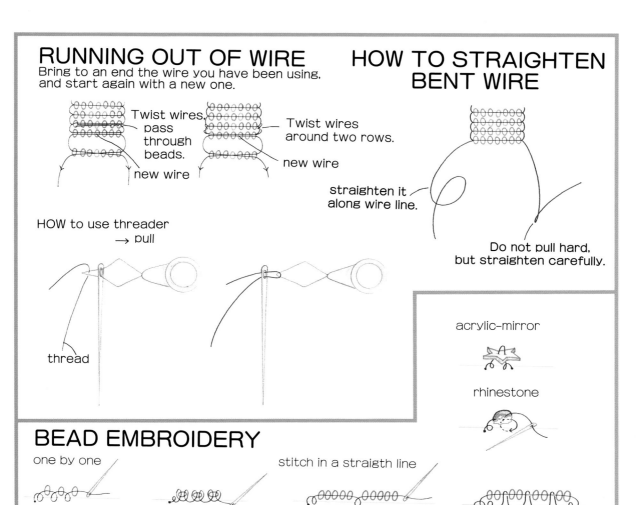

Twist wires, pass through beads.

new wire

Twist wires around two rows.

new wire

HOW TO STRAIGHTEN BENT WIRE

straighten it along wire line.

Do not pull hard, but straighten carefully.

HOW to use threader
→ pull

thread

acrylic-mirror

rhinestone

BEAD EMBROIDERY

one by one

stitch in a straigth line

USEFUL TOOLS

bead tray

scissors

tweezers

Pinch and sew three corners of 10cm (4″) X 10cm (4″) felt.

awl

white craft glue

wire crtter

pincers

thimble

PARTS FOR ACCESSORIES

barrette

comb

screw earringclips

carring clips

pin back

metal parts for ending jewelry

T-pin

clasps

jump Rings, spring ring, end br

LET'S PRACTICE

Start with the designs on these two pages. Learn how to make basic shapes, and then go on to make your own pieces.

A LITTLE GIRL

Materials

small cireular besds,
pearl beads (7mm),
wire 60cm (24″)

By substituting large beads
for the small ones you can
make a larger figure.

① Beginnig

Begin by stringing beads
in the middle of the wire.

②
a.
Tighten wire well.

b.
Tighten it well
again.

③
Tighten wire well.

④
Pass two wires
through blue bead,
tighten them well,
and then pass them

tighten them well.

⑤
Make skirt part by
tightening row by row.

⑥ Beginning

pearl (7mm)

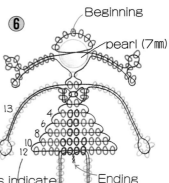

13
4
6
8
10
12
5

Numerals indicate
number of beads.

Ending
twist wire tight,
pass it through
bead and cut it.

3

4

1) Cut wire into length specified, start from "beginning," and put beads in the center of wire unless otherwire indecated. (The measurements include extra lengh to make your work easier.)

2) If you want to make a flat figure, like the girl on the opposite page, you have to cross wires from right and left in the beads. (The two crossing wires are illustrated as one wire in most cases.

3) Wires are illustrated as loose on purpose inorder to make the sequence clear, but when you work, you have to tighten wires each time you pass them through beads.

A CAP

(THREE-DIMENSIONAL FIGURE)

Materials

small circular beads, wire 60cm (24")

You can make a cap with vartical stripes by changing arrangement of colors.

① Beginning

(Leave 7cm (2¾") of wire to make ornament on top.)

② To the 2nd row.

The 1st row.
Pass wire through six beads.
Repeat six times to make a flower pattern.
Tighten wire each time.

③ To the 3rd row.

The 2nd row.
Pass wire through five beads
each time, and then through the bead which is in the center of the 1st row.

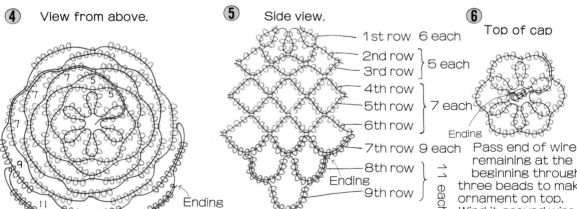

④ View from above.

Numerals indicate number of beads.

⑤ Side view.

1st row 6 each
2nd row ⎫
3rd row ⎬ 5 each
4th row ⎫
5th row ⎬ 7 each
6th row ⎭
7th row 9 each
8th row ⎫
Ending ⎬ 11 each
9th row ⎭

In this book, explanations are given up to the 2nd row as seen from above (or below), and then as seen from the side.

⑥ Top of cap

Ending

Pass end of wire remaining at the beginning through three beads to make ornament on top. Wind it around wire on other side, and then cut end.

LITTLE RED RIDING HOOD

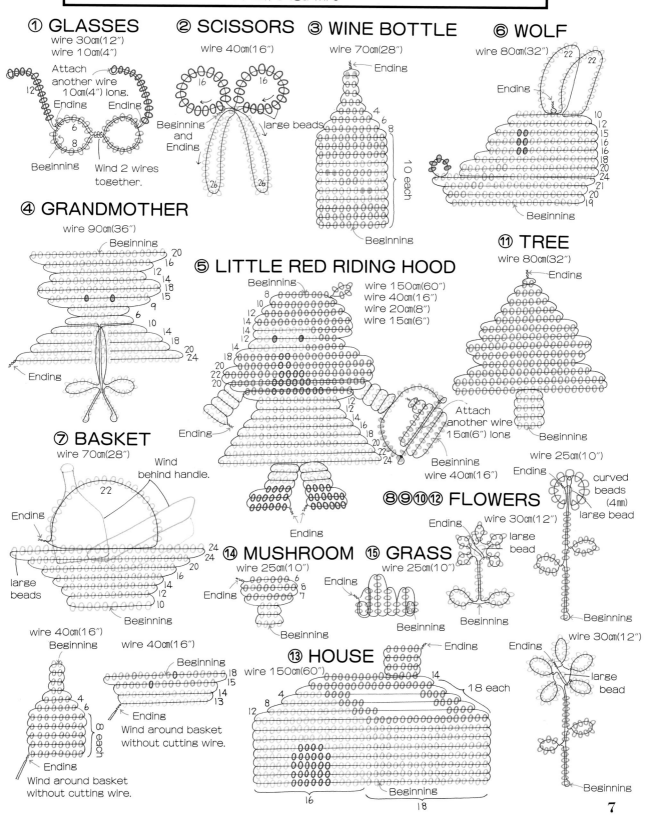

Designs ①-⑮   Use small beads unless otherwire indicated.
Materials : small circular beads, large circular baeds,
curved baeds (4mm), 34ga wire

① GLASSES
wire 30cm(12")
wire 10cm(4")
Attach another wire 10cm(4") long.
12
Ending   Ending
6
8
Beginning   Wind 2 wires together.

② SCISSORS
wire 40cm(16")
16   16
Beginning and Ending
large beads
26   26

③ WINE BOTTLE
wire 70cm(28")
Ending
4
6
8
10 each
Beginning

⑥ WOLF
wire 80cm(32")
22   22
Ending
10
12
15
16
16
18
20
24
21
20
19
Beginning

④ GRANDMOTHER
wire 90cm(36")
Beginning
20
16
12
14
18
15
9
6
10
14
18
20
24
Ending

⑤ LITTLE RED RIDING HOOD
Beginning
8
10
12
14
14
12
14
18
20
22
20
Ending
wire 150cm(60")
wire 40cm(16")
wire 20cm(8")
wire 15cm(6")
12
14
16
18
20
22
24
Attach another wire 15cm(6") long
Beginning wire 40cm(16")

⑪ TREE
wire 80cm(32")
Ending
Beginning
wire 25cm(10")
Ending
curved beads (4mm)
large bead

⑦ BASKET
wire 70cm(28")
Wind behind handle.
22
Ending
large beads
24
24
20
16
14
12
10
Beginning

⑧⑨⑩⑫ FLOWERS
Ending
large bead
wire 30cm(12")
Beginning

⑭ MUSHROOM
wire 25cm(10")
6
6
7
Ending
Beginning

⑮ GRASS
wire 25cm(10")
Ending
Beginning   Beginning

Ending   large bead
wire 30cm(12")
Ending
large bead
Beginning

wire 40cm(16")
Beginning
4
6
8 each
Ending
Wind around basket without cutting wire.

wire 40cm(16")
Beginning
18
15
14
13
Ending
Wind around basket without cutting wire.

⑬ HOUSE
wire 150cm(60")
Ending
14
4
8
12
18 each
Beginning
16   18

7

THUMBELINA

Designs ①-⑬   Use small beads unless otherwse indicated.
Materials : small circular beads, large circular beads, tulle lace,
bugle beads (3mm) (6mm), bells 1.4cm(5/8") in diameter, 31ga wire

① SWALLOW

wire 70cm(28")
2 wires 50cm(20")

Ending

6 6 5

4 5 5 6 6

7 each

Ending

Beginning
wire 50cm(20")

4 5

② PRINCE

wire 120cm(48")

Ending

elliptic tulle lace
9cm(3 5/8") × 5cm(2")
5cm(2") ×1.5cm(5/8")

10
11
13
15
13
11
13
10
11
9
7
9
7
9
13

Beginning
wire
70cm(28")

7 each

6
6
8
12

Beginning

Wring
the center of
elliptic tulle lace.
make
gatherings,
and fix it
at the back.

③ THUMBELINA

wire 150cm(60")
tulle lace
24cm(9 5/8")   5cm(2")

pass wire through
holes of tulle lace,
make gathering.

Ending

8
10
13
15
15
12
10
9
8
8
8
8
14
17
19
21
24
26
27
28
29
30
30

wire 20cm(8")

★ ★ ★
★   ★

Beginning

⑪ TURTLE

for a large tutle
wire 50cm(20")
large beads
for a small tutle
e 40cm(16")

Beginning
8   8

Ending

⑥ THUMBELINA

wire 100cm(40")
wire 20cm(8")

Ending

8
12
14
12
9

13
15
17
19
21
22
23

Beginning

Ending

6

4

Attach
another wire
20cm(8") long

⑦ MOLE

wire 80cm(32")
wire 50cm(20")

10 10
6   8
6
6

large bead

Ending

Beginning
wire 50cm(20")

8
13
14
17
18
17
13

12
13

Beginning

⑧ MOUSE

wire 100cm(40")
wire 50cm(20")

10 11 11   8
Beginning 5
5

9

7

large beads

Ending

Ending

7
8
10

11
16
17
18
20
23
24
25
27

Beginning

10

5

15

⑨ FROG

wire 60cm(24")

large beads

Ending

10
12
13
13

13

Beginning

⑫ FISH

wire 80cm(32")

15
12 14 14 14 13   13
11   8
6   5   4
large   4   12
bead
5   6

Beginning

Ending

Return by winding
wire around.

⑩ TULIPS

wire 50cm(20")
2 wires 30cm(12")
2 wires 20cm(8")

Ending

Attach
another wire
20cm(8") long

Ending

9
8
8
8

5 5
5 7 7
7
4

Beginning

Beginning

Attach another wire
30cm(12") long
to each place

⑬ CRAYFISH

wire 70cm(28")
2 wires 30cm(12")

bugle
beads
(3mm)
Ending

Beginning

large
beads

Attach
another wire
30cm(12") long
to each place.

Ending

⑤ BUTTERFLY

2 wires 70cm(28") 3 wires 30cm(12")

bugle beads
(6mm)

wire 30cm(12")
Beginning

Attach another wire
70cm(28") long
to each place

8
10
16 14 12
4
5
4 5

Ending

Attach
another wire
30cm(12") long
to each place

large bead

④ WEDDING BELL

Ending

wire 60cm(24")
large
beads

10 9 7 6 4
5

Beginning

Bells
1.4cm(5/8")

Ending

9

Designs ①-⑲   Use small beads unless otherwise indicated.
Materials : small circular beads, large circular beads, curved beads (3mm) (4mm) (5mm), bugle beads (6mm), pearl beads (2mm) (2.5mm) (5mm) (6mm), small star-shaped spangle, large star-shaped spangle, leaf-shaped parts, 34ga wire

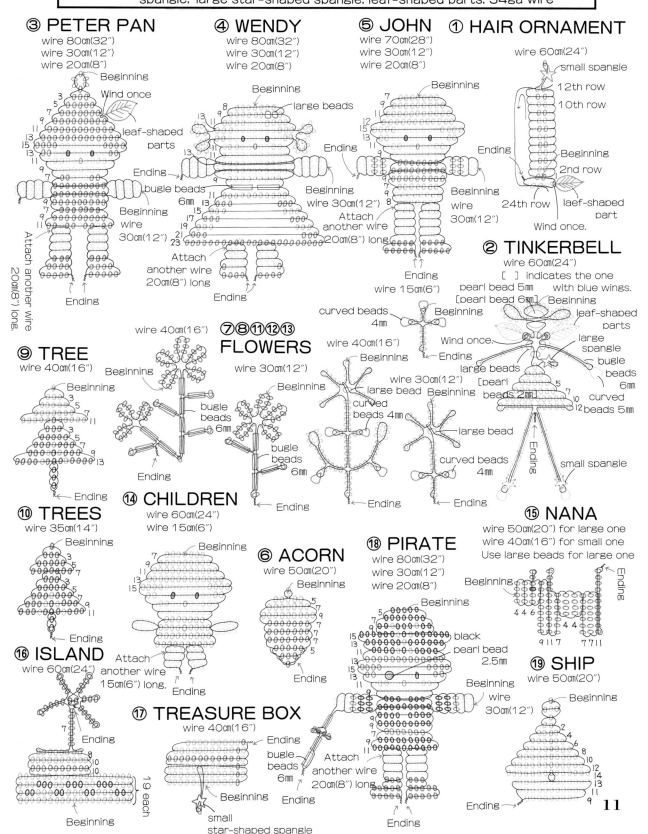

③ PETER PAN
wire 80cm(32")
wire 30cm(12")
wire 20cm(8")
Beginning
Wind once
leaf-shaped parts
bugle beads 6mm
Beginning wire 30cm(12")
Attach another wire 20cm(8") long.
Ending

④ WENDY
wire 80cm(32")
wire 30cm(12")
wire 20cm(8")
Beginning
large beads
Ending
bugle beads 6mm
Beginning wire 30cm(12")
Attach another wire 20cm(8") long
Ending

⑤ JOHN
wire 70cm(28")
wire 30cm(12")
wire 20cm(8")
Beginning
Beginning wire 30cm(12")
Attach another wire 20cm(8") long
Ending
wire 15cm(6")

① HAIR ORNAMENT
wire 60cm(24")
small spangle
12th row
10th row
Ending
Beginning
2nd row
24th row
laef-shaped part
Wind once.

② TINKERBELL
wire 60cm(24")
[ ] indicates the one with blue wings.
pearl bead 5mm
[pearl bead 6mm]
Beginning
leaf-shaped parts
large spangle
bugle beads 6mm
large beads
[pearl beads 2mm]
curved beads 5mm
Ending
small spangle

⑨ TREE
wire 40cm(16")
Beginning
Ending

⑦⑧⑪⑫⑬ FLOWERS
wire 40cm(16")
Beginning
bugle beads 6mm
wire 30cm(12")
Beginning
bugle beads 6mm
Ending

curved beads 4mm
Beginning
Ending
wire 40cm(16")
Beginning
large bead
curved beads 4mm
wire 30cm(12")
Beginning
large bead
curved beads 4mm
Ending   Ending

⑩ TREES
wire 35cm(14")
Beginning
Ending

⑭ CHILDREN
wire 60cm(24")
wire 15cm(6")
Beginning
Attach another wire 15cm(6") long.
Ending

⑥ ACORN
wire 50cm(20")
Beginning
Ending

⑱ PIRATE
wire 80cm(32")
wire 30cm(12")
wire 20cm(8")
Beginning
Beginning
black pearl bead 2.5mm
Beginning wire 30cm(12")
Attach another wire 20cm(8") long
Ending

⑮ NANA
wire 50cm(20") for large one
wire 40cm(16") for small one
Use large beads for large one
Beginning
Ending

⑯ ISLAND
wire 60cm(24")
Ending
Beginning
19 each

⑰ TREASURE BOX
wire 40cm(16")
Ending
bugle beads 6mm
Beginning
small star-shaped spangle
Ending

⑲ SHIP
wire 50cm(20")
Beginning
Ending

11

THE WOLF AND SEVEN LITTLE KIDS

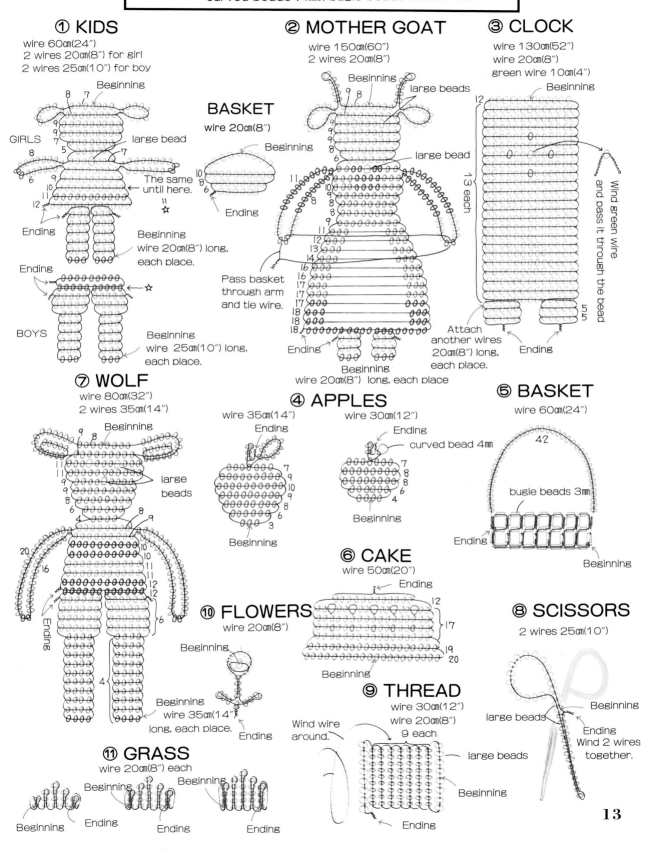

Designs ①-⑪   Use small beads unless otherwise indicated.
Materials : small cirular beads, large circular beads,
           curved beads (4mm), bugle beads (3mm), 34ga wire

① KIDS
wire 60cm(24")
2 wires 20cm(8") for girl
2 wires 25cm(10") for boy

BASKET
wire 20cm(8")

② MOTHER GOAT
wire 150cm(60")
2 wires 20cm(8")

③ CLOCK
wire 130cm(52")
wire 20cm(8")
green wire 10cm(4")

Beginning

GIRLS
large bead
The same until here.

Beginning
wire 20cm(8") long,
each place.

Ending

Ending

BOYS

Beginning
wire 25cm(10") long,
each place.

large beads

Beginning
Beginning

Ending

large bead

Pass basket through arm and tie wire.

Ending

Beginning
wire 20cm(8") long, each place

13 each

Wind green wire and pass it through the bead

Beginning

Attach another wires 20cm(8") long, each place.

Ending

⑦ WOLF
wire 80cm(32")
2 wires 35cm(14")

Beginning

large beads

Beginning
wire 35cm(14") long, each place.

Ending

④ APPLES
wire 35cm(14")

wire 30cm(12")

Ending

Ending
curved bead 4mm

Beginning

Beginning

⑤ BASKET
wire 60cm(24")

42

bugle beads 3mm

Ending

Beginning

⑥ CAKE
wire 50cm(20")

Ending

Beginning

⑧ SCISSORS
2 wires 25cm(10")

⑩ FLOWERS
wire 20cm(8")

⑨ THREAD
wire 30cm(12")
wire 20cm(8")
9 each

large beads

Beginning

Ending
Wind 2 wires together.

Wind wire around.

large beads

Beginning

Ending

⑪ GRASS
wire 20cm(8") each

Beginning

Beginning

Beginning

Beginning

Ending

Beginning

Ending

Ending

13

PUSS IN BOOTS

Designs ①-⑬ Use small beads unless otherwise indicated.
Materials : small circular beads, large circular beads, curved beads (3mm),
small hexagonal beads, pearl beads (3mm) (4mm) (8mm), oval pearl
beads (3×6mm), miniatures of grapes, 31ga wire

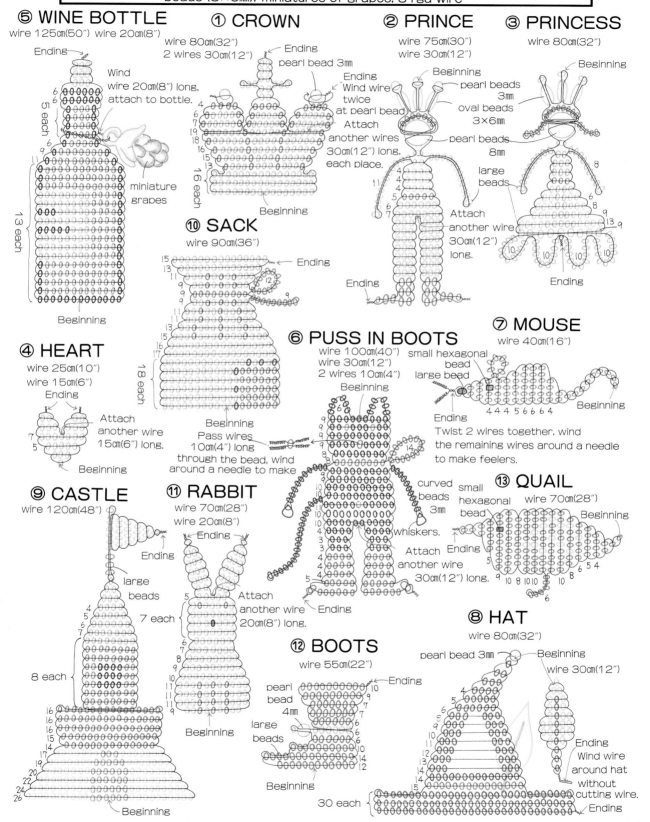

⑤ WINE BOTTLE
wire 125cm(50") wire 20cm(8")

Ending
Wind wire 20cm(8") long, attach to bottle.
6 each
5 each
13 each
miniature grapes
Beginning

① CROWN
wire 80cm(32")
2 wires 30cm(12")
Ending
pearl bead 3mm
4
7
19
18
16
13
13
16 each
Beginning

② PRINCE
wire 75cm(30")
wire 30cm(12")
Beginning
Ending
Wind wire twice at pearl bead
Attach another wires 30cm(12") long, each place.
4
4
4
6
7
Attach another wire 30cm(12") long.
Ending

③ PRINCESS
wire 80cm(32")
Beginning
pearl beads 3mm
oval beads 3×6mm
pearl beads 8mm
large beads
8
8
9
13 9
10 10 10 10
Ending

⑩ SACK
wire 90cm(36")
15
11
15
9
9
12
Ending
13
15
16
17
18 each
Beginning
Pass wires 10cm(4") long through the bead, wind around a needle to make

④ HEART
wire 25cm(10")
wire 15cm(6")
Ending
7
5
Attach another wire 15cm(6") long.
Beginning

⑥ PUSS IN BOOTS
wire 100cm(40")
wire 30cm(12")
2 wires 10cm(4")
Beginning
9
9
9
9
9
10
10
10
10
4
3
5
4
4
4
14
curved beads 3mm
whiskers.
Attach another wire 30cm(12") long.
Ending

⑦ MOUSE
wire 40cm(16")
small hexagonal bead
large bead
Ending
4 4 4 5 6 6 6 4
Beginning
Twist 2 wires together, wind the remaining wires around a needle to make feelers.

⑬ QUAIL
wire 70cm(28")
small hexagonal bead
Ending
Beginning
10 8 10 10
6 5 4
10
6

⑨ CASTLE
wire 120cm(48")
Ending
large beads
4
6
7
8 each
16
16
16
15
14
17
19
20
22
24
26
Beginning

⑪ RABBIT
wire 70cm(28")
wire 20cm(8")
Ending
7 each
5
Attach another wire 20cm(8") long.
Ending
8
10
11
9
11
9
Beginning

⑫ BOOTS
wire 55cm(22")
10
10
9
7
pearl bead 4mm
large beads
6
6
14
12
Ending
Beginning

⑧ HAT
wire 80cm(32")
pearl bead 3mm
Beginning
wire 30cm(12")
5
4
6
10
10
12
14
14
15
30 each
Ending
Wind wire around hat without cutting wire.
Ending

15

AWAY WE GO

16

Designs ①–⑬   Use large beads unless otherwise indicated.
Materials : small circular beads, large circular beads, curved beads (4mm),
oval pearl beads (3×6mm), bugle beads (3mm) (6mm), 31ga wire

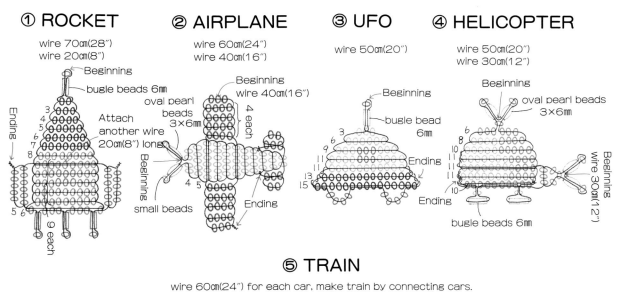

① ROCKET
wire 70cm(28″)
wire 20cm(8″)

- Beginning
- bugle beads 6mm
- Attach another wire 20cm(8″) long
- Ending
- 3 4 5 6 7 8
- 5 6
- 9 each

② AIRPLANE
wire 60cm(24″)
wire 40cm(16″)

- Beginning wire 40cm(16″)
- oval pearl beads 3×6mm
- 4 each
- Beginning
- small beads
- 4 5
- Ending

③ UFO
wire 50cm(20″)

- Beginning
- bugle bead 6mm
- 6 3
- 9
- 11 11 13 15
- Ending

④ HELICOPTER
wire 50cm(20″)
wire 30cm(12″)

- Beginning
- oval pearl beads 3×6mm
- 8 10
- 11 11
- 10
- Beginning wire 30cm(12″)
- Ending
- bugle beads 6mm

⑤ TRAIN
wire 60cm(24″) for each car, make train by connecting cars.

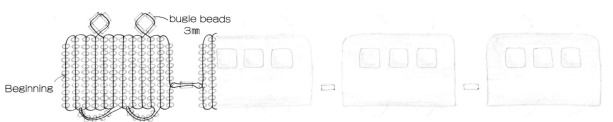

- bugle beads 3mm
- Beginning

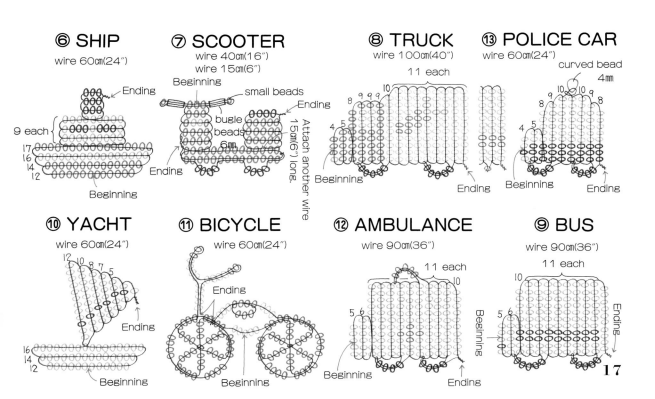

⑥ SHIP
wire 60cm(24″)

- Ending
- 9 each
- 17 16 14 12
- Beginning

⑦ SCOOTER
wire 40cm(16″)
wire 15cm(6″)

- Beginning
- small beads
- Ending
- bugle beads 6mm
- Attach another wire 15cm(6″) long.
- Ending

⑧ TRUCK
wire 100cm(40″)

- 11 each
- 10
- 8 9 9 9
- 4 5
- Beginning
- Ending

⑬ POLICE CAR
wire 60cm(24″)

- curved bead 4mm
- 10 10
- 8 9 9 8
- 4 5
- Beginning
- Ending

⑩ YACHT
wire 60cm(24″)

- 12 10 8 7 5
- Ending
- 16 14 12
- Beginning

⑪ BICYCLE
wire 60cm(24″)

- Ending
- Beginning

⑫ AMBULANCE
wire 90cm(36″)

- 11 each
- 10
- 5 6
- Beginning
- Ending

⑨ BUS
wire 90cm(36″)

- 11 each
- 10
- 5 6
- Beginning
- Ending

17

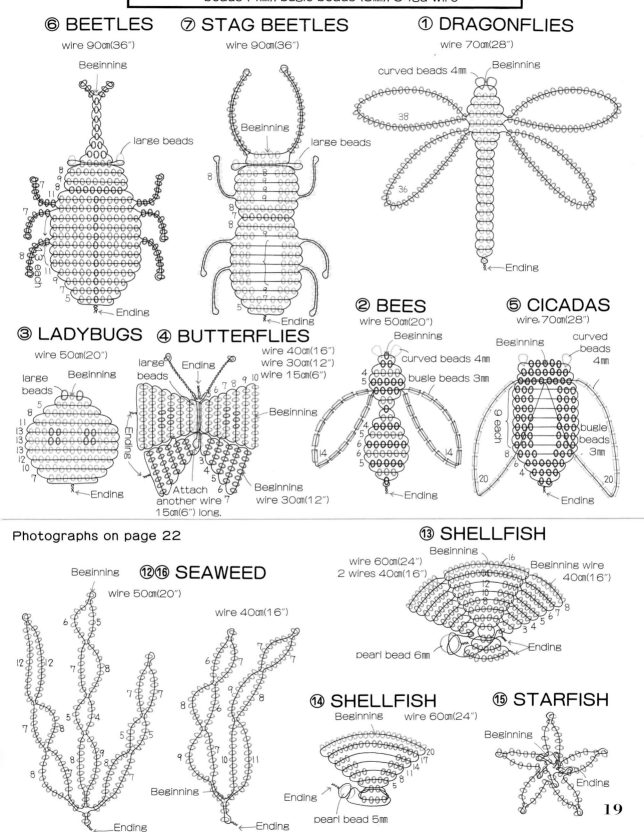

Designs ①–⑦   Use small beads unless otherwise indicated.
Materials : small circular beads, large circular beads, curved beads (4㎜), bugle beads (3㎜), 34ga wire

⑥ BEETLES
wire 90㎝(36")
Beginning
large beads
13 each
Ending

⑦ STAG BEETLES
wire 90㎝(36")
Beginning
large beads
Ending

① DRAGONFLIES
wire 70㎝(28")
curved beads 4㎜
Beginning
38
36
Ending

③ LADYBUGS
wire 50㎝(20")
large beads
Beginning
Ending

④ BUTTERFLIES
wire 40㎝(16")
wire 30㎝(12")
wire 15㎝(6")
large beads
Ending
Beginning
Beginning
wire 30㎝(12")
Attach another wire 15㎝(6") long.

② BEES
wire 50㎝(20")
Beginning
curved beads 4㎜
bugle beads 3㎜
Ending

⑤ CICADAS
wire 70㎝(28")
Beginning
curved beads 4㎜
9 each
bugle beads 3㎜
Ending

Photographs on page 22

⑫⑯ SEAWEED
Beginning
wire 50㎝(20")
wire 40㎝(16")
Beginning
Ending
Ending

⑬ SHELLFISH
wire 60㎝(24")
2 wires 40㎝(16")
Beginning
Beginning wire 40㎝(16")
pearl bead 6㎜
Ending

⑭ SHELLFISH
Beginning   wire 60㎝(24")
Ending
pearl bead 5㎜

⑮ STARFISH
Beginning
Ending

19

KITCHEN CHARMS

Designs ①-⑱   Use small beads unless otherwise indicated.
Materials : small circular beads, bugle beads (9mm), 31ga wire

④ WINE GLASSES
wire 50cm(20″)
11 each
10
7
Ending
bugle beas 9mm
7
9
Beginning

⑤ PEPPER
wire 60cm(24″)
5
5
5
Ending
7
8
9
10
11
12
13
14
15
Beginning

⑥ SALT
wire 60cm(24″)
6
6
Ending
7
8
9
10
11
12
13
14
15
Beginning

① MUG
wire 70cm(28″)
15 each
18
Ending
Beginning

③ FRYPAN
wire 100cm(40″)
Ending
4 each
3
13
16
9
16
13
9
21 each
Beginning

⑩ SPOON
wire 40cm(16″)
Beginning
3
5
7
8
8
7
5
Ending

⑨ FORK
wire 40cm(16″)
Ending
7
5 each

⑪ CUPCAKE
wire 70cm(28″)
Ending
19
15 each
25
22
Beginning

② POT
wire 100cm(40″)
17
20
22
8
10
22
20 each
Ending
Beginning

⑭ TEACUP
wire 50cm(20″)
15
13
12
11
10
9
Ending
20
18
Ending
Beginning

⑦ EGGPLANT
wire 50cm(20″)
Ending
4
5
7
8
8
10
10
7
5
Beginning

⑧ CARROT
wire 60cm(24″)
Ending
10
9
8
7
6
5
4
3
Beginning

⑬ KETTLE
wire 90cm(36″)
wire 20cm(8″)
35
7
Ending
8
12
14
15
16
17
18
19
20
20
Beginning
Ending

⑮ TEAPOT
wire 90cm(36″)
wire 20cm(8″)
Beginning
wire 20cm(8″)
5
7
8
10
20
11
12
13
14
15
3
3
4
6
16
17
17
16
Ending
Ending
Beginning

⑯ RADISH
wire 80cm(32″)
10
10
10
10
8
9
8
7
6
5
4
3
Ending
Beginning

⑰ JAM
wire 70cm(28″)
13
13
Ending
15 each
Beginning

⑱ TOAST
wire 50cm(20″)
13
6
10
8
9
10
11
11
12
Ending
Beginning

⑫ WATERMELON
wire 70cm(28″)
10 each
24
23
22
21
20
17
15
12
Ending
Beginning

21

SEA LIFE

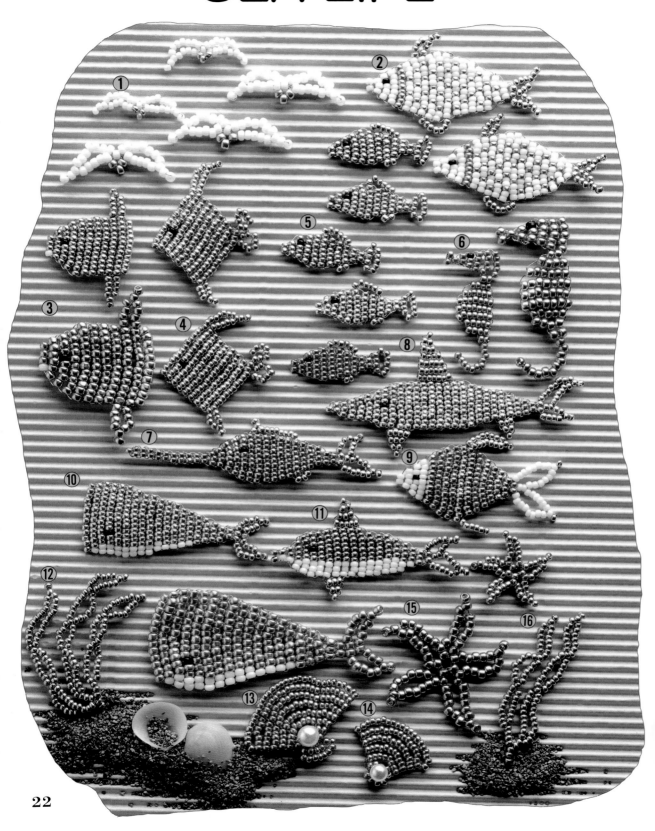

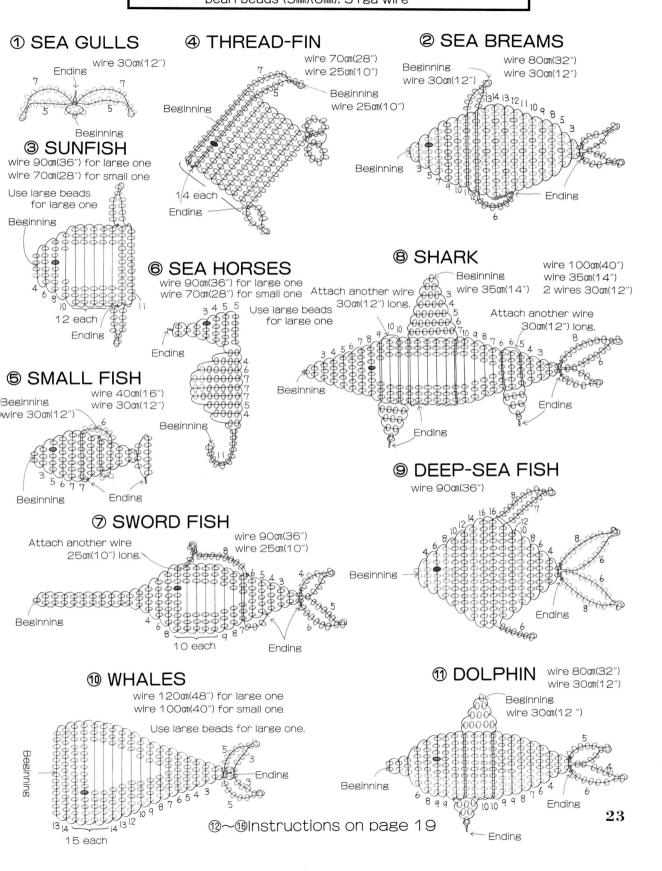

Designs ①-⑯　　Use small beads unless otherwise indicated.
Materials : small circular beads, large circular beads,
pearl beads (5mm)(6mm), 31ga wire

① SEA GULLS
wire 30cm(12″)
Ending
Beginning

③ SUNFISH
wire 90cm(36″) for large one
wire 70cm(28″) for small one

Use large beads for large one
Beginning
12 each
Ending

⑤ SMALL FISH
wire 40cm(16″)
wire 30cm(12″)
Beginning
wire 30cm(12″)
Beginning
Ending

④ THREAD-FIN
wire 70cm(28″)
wire 25cm(10″)
Beginning
wire 25cm(10″)
Beginning
1/4 each
Ending

⑥ SEA HORSES
wire 90cm(36″) for large one
wire 70cm(28″) for small one
Use large beads for large one
Ending
Beginning
Beginning

⑦ SWORD FISH
Attach another wire 25cm(10″) long.
wire 90cm(36″)
wire 25cm(10″)
Beginning
10 each
Ending

② SEA BREAMS
wire 80cm(32″)
wire 30cm(12″)
Beginning
wire 30cm(12″)
Beginning
Ending

⑧ SHARK
wire 100cm(40″)
wire 35cm(14″)
2 wires 30cm(12″)
Beginning
wire 35cm(14″)
Attach another wire 30cm(12″) long.
Attach another wire 30cm(12″) long.
Beginning
Ending
Ending

⑨ DEEP-SEA FISH
wire 90cm(36″)
Beginning
Ending

⑩ WHALES
wire 120cm(48″) for large one
wire 100cm(40″) for small one.
Use large beads for large one.
Beginning
Ending
15 each

⑪ DOLPHIN
wire 80cm(32″)
wire 30cm(12″)
Beginning
wire 30cm(12″)
Beginning
Ending
Ending

⑫～⑯Instructions on page 19

23

12 SIGNS OF THE ZODIAC

Instructions on page 48.

24

① ② ③ ④ ⑤ ⑥ ⑦ ⑧ ⑨ ⑩ ⑪ ⑫ ㉗

PATTERN (actual size)

Cut out felt.

Draw face with felt-tip pen.

Cut out doll after sticking felt on cardboard.

Make two braids and tie with bows of embroidery floss as in photo on page 27.

③ POLO SHIRT

wire 110cm(44″)
wire 50cm(20″)
2 wires 40cm(16″)
2 wires 30cm(12″)

Attach another wire 50cm(20″) long.

Attach another wire 30cm(12″) long.

Ending

Beginning wire 45cm(18″)

4 3
5
6
6
7

19 each   Beginning

⑥ SWEATER

wire 110cm(44″)
2 wires 60cm(24″)
wire 50cm(20″)

Attach another wire 50cm(20″) long.

Ending

Beginning wire 60cm(24″) long.

3
4
5
6
6

7 each

6

19 each   Beginning

Ending

⑦ BOOK BAG

Ending

wire 50cm(20″)

8 each

Beginning

⑮ TUXEDO, ㉒ JACKET

wire 140cm(56″)
2 wires 60cm(24″)

Use only black brads for jacket, except for gold beads at center 2 rows apart.

Ending

Beginning wire 60cm(24″)

4 3
5
6
6
7 each

20 each   Beginning   Ending

㉓ SCHOOL BAG

5 each, repeat 46 times

Ending

20 each

small beads wire 160cm(64″)

Beginning

⑰ TOP

Attach another wire 50cm(20″) long.

wire 100cm(40″)
wire 50cm(20″)

Ending

6
7
8

6

19 each

9 each

6

Beginning

⑧ JEANS, ⑯ PANTS

wire 140cm(56″)
wire 90cm(36″)

Beginning

19 each

9 each

Attach another wire 90cm(36″) long.

9 each

wire 70cm(28″)
wire 40cm(16″)

8 each

Attach another wire 40cm(16″) long.

7 each

Ending

④⑱ SHORTS

wire 70cm(28″)
wire 30cm(12″)

Beginning

6

19 each

9 each

6

Attach another wire 30cm(12″) long.

Ending

⑭ SWIM TRUNKS

small beads

Beginning

8

22 each

11 each

8

Attach another wire 40cm(16″) long

Ending   Ending   Ending

28

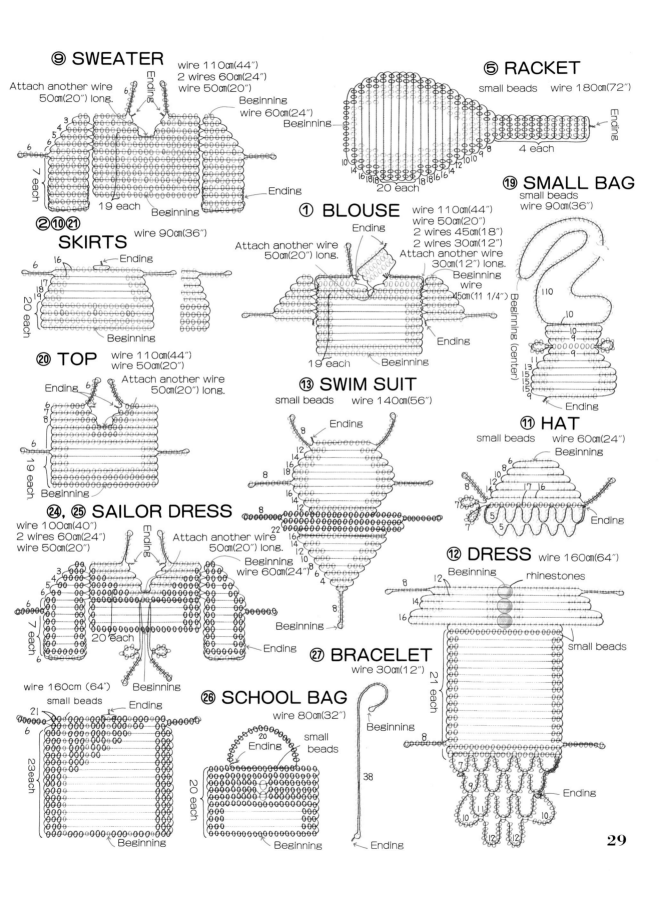

DOLL HOUSE
FURNITURE

⑬ ⑭ ⑯ ⑰ ⑮ ⑱

Designs ①-⑱   Use small beads unless otherwise indicated.
Materials : small circular beads, large circular beads, extra large circular beads,
pearl beads (4㎜)(6㎜), oval pearl beads (3×6㎜), curved beads, bugle beads (6㎜),
31ga wire, ribbon, cardboard, craft glue.

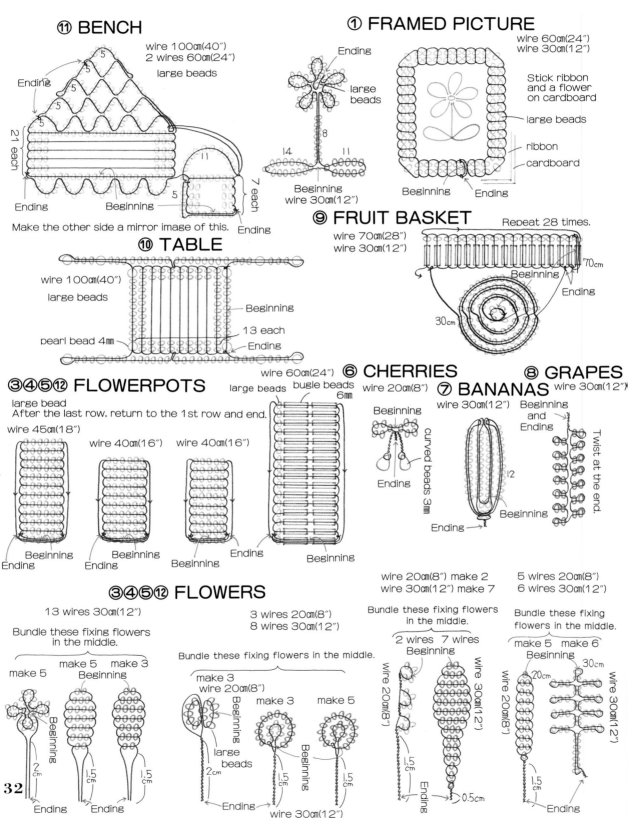

⑪ BENCH

wire 100㎝(40")
2 wires 60㎝(24")
large beads

Ending

21 each

Ending   Beginning

7 each

Ending

Make the other side a mirror image of this.   Ending

① FRAMED PICTURE

Ending

large beads

wire 60㎝(24")
wire 30㎝(12")

Stick ribbon
and a flower
on cardboard

large beads

ribbon

cardboard

Beginning   Ending

Beginning
wire 30㎝(12")

⑩ TABLE

wire 100㎝(40")

large beads

pearl bead 4㎜

Beginning

13 each

Ending

⑨ FRUIT BASKET

Repeat 28 times.

wire 70㎝(28")
wire 30㎝(12")

70㎝

Beginning

Ending

30㎝

③④⑤⑫ FLOWERPOTS

large bead
After the last row, return to the 1st row and end.

wire 45㎝(18")

wire 40㎝(16")   wire 40㎝(16")

wire 60㎝(24")
large beads   bugle beads
6㎜

Ending   Beginning

Beginning   Beginning
Ending   Ending   Beginning   Beginning

⑥ CHERRIES

wire 20㎝(8")

Beginning

curved beads 3㎜

Ending

⑦ BANANAS

wire 30㎝(12")

12

Beginning

Ending

⑧ GRAPES

wire 30㎝(12")

Beginning
and
Ending

Twist at the end.

③④⑤⑫ FLOWERS

13 wires 30㎝(12")

Bundle these fixing flowers
in the middle.

make 5

make 5   make 3
Beginning

Beginning

2
㎝

Ending

Beginning

1.5
㎝

Ending

1.5
㎝

Ending

3 wires 20㎝(8")
8 wires 30㎝(12")

Bundle these fixing flowers in the middle.

make 3
wire 20㎝(8")

make 3   make 5

large
beads

Beginning

2㎝

Beginning

1.5
㎝

Ending

Beginning

1.5
㎝

Ending

wire 30㎝(12")

wire 20㎝(8") make 2
wire 30㎝(12") make 7

Bundle these fixing flowers
in the middle.

2 wires   7 wires
Beginning

wire 20㎝(8")

wire 30㎝(12")

1.5
㎝

Ending

0.5㎝

5 wires 20㎝(8")
6 wires 30㎝(12")

Bundle these fixing
flowers in the middle.

make 5   make 6
Beginning

20㎝   30㎝

wire 20㎝(8")

wire 30㎝(12")

1.5
㎝

Ending

32

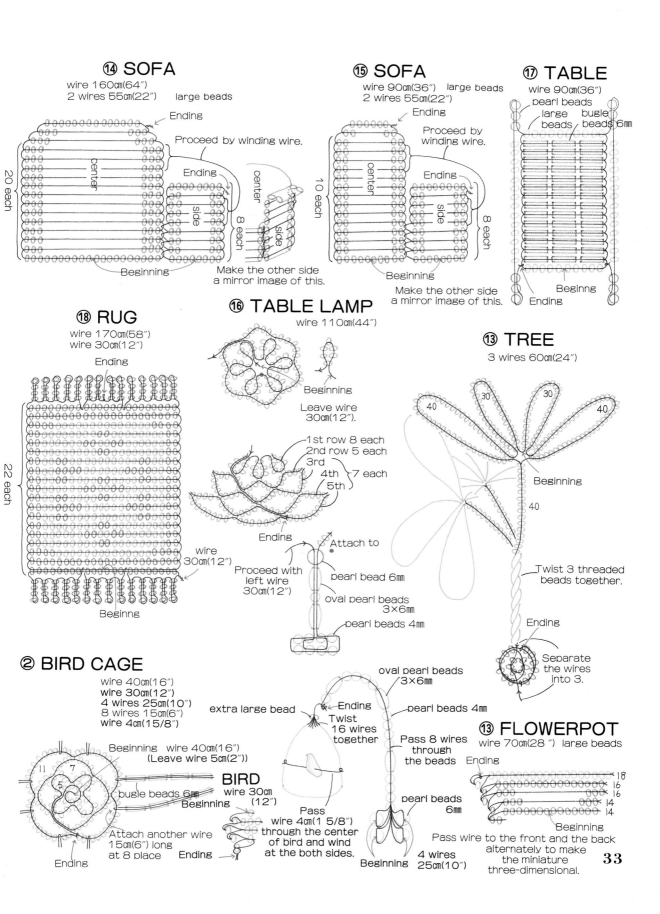

⑭ SOFA
wire 160cm(64")
2 wires 55cm(22")   large beads

Ending

Proceed by winding wire.

Ending

center

20 each

side

8 each

center

side

Beginning

Make the other side
a mirror image of this.

⑮ SOFA
wire 90cm(36")   large beads
2 wires 55cm(22")

Ending

Proceed by
winding wire.

Ending

center

10 each

side

8 each

Beginning

Make the other side
a mirror image of this.

⑰ TABLE
wire 90cm(36")
pearl beads
large   bugle
beads   beads 6mm

Beginng

Ending

⑱ RUG
wire 170cm(58")
wire 30cm(12")

Ending

22 each

center

wire
30cm(12")

Beginng

⑯ TABLE LAMP
wire 110cm(44")

Beginning

Leave wire
30cm(12").

1st row 8 each
2nd row 5 each
3rd
4th   7 each
5th

Ending

Attach to

Proceed with
left wire
30cm(12")

pearl bead 6mm

oval pearl beads
3×6mm

pearl beads 4mm

⑬ TREE
3 wires 60cm(24")

30   30
40   40

Beginning

40

Twist 3 threaded
beads together.

Ending

Separate
the wires
into 3.

② BIRD CAGE
wire 40cm(16")
wire 30cm(12")
4 wires 25cm(10")
8 wires 15cm(6")
wire 4cm(15/8")

extra large bead

Beginning wire 40cm(16")
(Leave wire 5cm(2"))

11   7
5

bugle beads 6mm

BIRD
wire 30cm
(12")

Beginning

Attach another wire
15cm(6") long
at 8 place

Ending

Pass
wire 4cm(1 5/8")
through the center
of bird and wind
at the both sides.

Ending

oval pearl beads
3×6mm

Ending
Twist
16 wires
together

pearl beads 4mm

Pass 8 wires
through
the beads

pearl beads
6mm

Beginning

4 wires
25cm(10")

⑬ FLOWERPOT
wire 70cm(28") large beads

Ending

18
16
16
14
14

Beginning

Pass wire to the front and the back
alternately to make
the miniature
three-dimensional.

33

① ② ③ ④ ⑤ ⑥ ⑦

Designs ①-⑬   Use small beads unless otherwise indicated.
Materials : small circular beads, large circular beads, curved beads (3mm)(4mm),
bugle beads (9mm), 31ga wire, small hexagonal beads, large hexagonal
beads, miniatures of banana

wire 170cm(68")
(wire 130cm(52"))
wire 100cm(40")   for large one.
(wire 70cm(28"))   for small one.
Use large beads for large one.
[ ] indicates the small one.
curved beads 3mm
[small hexagonal bead]

① ELEPHANTS

Make ear with wire on the other side,
Ending   wind around body.

Beginnng
wire 100cm(40")
[wire 70cm(28")]

Beginnng
wire 170cm(68")
[wire 130cm(52")]
large bead
curved bead 4mm
[curved bead 3mm]

Beginning
(center on the
other side).
wire 50cm(20")

Ending

Ending

⑧ BEAR

wire 90cm(36")
wire 50cm(20")

Make leg on the out side.

Beginning wire 90cm(36")

Ending

Ending

Pass wire to front and to back
alternately to make miniature
three-dimensional.

⑦ RABBITS

Ending
wire 85cm(34")
wire 20cm(8")
wire 10cm(4")

Attach another wire
10cm(4") long.

Beginning

Attach another
wire 20cm(8")
long.

Pass wire to front and to back
alternately to make miniature
three-dimensional.

③ MONKEYS

wire 80cm(31")

9 each
Ending
Beginning
large bead

miniature banana

Pass wire to
the front and
to back alternately
to make miniature
three-dimensional.

⑩ GOATS

wire 100cm(40")

Ending   7each

curved bead 3mm

Beginning

Make another
horn and ear
on the other
side.

Pass wire to
front and to
back alternately
to make miniature
three-dimensional.

⑤ GIRAFFES

wire 90cm(36")   [wire 60cm(24")]
wire 80cm(32")   [wire 50cm(20")]
wire 40cm(16")   [wire 30cm(12")]
wire 15cm(6")   [ ] indicates the small one..
Use large beads for large one.

Ending
pearl bead
(3mm)

Attach another wire
15cm(6") long.

View from above.

Ending

Make legs
on the other side.

Beginning
wire 40cm(16")
[wire 30cm(12")]

curved bead 4mm
[curved bead 3mm]

Beginning
wire 90cm(36")
[wire 60cm(24")]

In the 1st row 10 each,
repeat 5 times.

Make ear and horns
on the other side.

Front view

Attach another wire
80cm(32") long.
[wire 50cm(20")]

Ending

Proced in this order;
body-neck-face-horn-
ear-mane-tail-leg.

Pass wire to front and
to back alternately
to make body, neck
and face
three-dimensional.

⑫ FENCES

wire 150cm(60")

Repeat 18 times

Ending   bugle beads
9mm

8   8

Beginning

⑨ TRASH CAN   wire 80cm(32")

Leave wire 5cm(2"), wind around the center.

7th row 5 each
6th row
5th row
4th row   7 each
3rd row
2nd row 5 each

2nd row, 5 each
1st row,
in the center
repeat 5 times.

1st row 10 each

④ FOUNTAIN

wire 65cm(26″)
wire 45cm(18″)

curved beads 4mm

Beginning

18

Pass wire to front and
to back alternately
to make miniature
three-dimensional.

10 large beads

8 each

★

20

20

20

20

Ending
Twist with ★

⑪ TULIPS

wire 30cm(12″)
2 wires 20cm(8″)

Pass wire through 10 beads,
make 4 of them.

Ending
Twist 4 wires
together.

large beads

Beginning

Attach another
wires 20cm(8″) long
each place.

② TREES

3 wires 60cm(24″)

Beginning

20

20

20

14

large beads

miniature
banana

27

large beads

10

10

10

10

Ending
Bundle 6 wires,
twist together.

⑬ FLAMINGO

wire 70cm(28″)
wire 150cm(60″)

small hexagonal bead

Beginning

Pass through
to other side.

Make tail with wire
on the other side.

Ending

Beginning

Beginning

Ending

Ending

Pass wire to front
and to back alternately
to make miniature
three-dimensional.

⑥ HIPPOPOTAMUS

wire 150cm(60″)
wire 70cm(28″)

Make ear with wire on the other side
wind wire around body.

large
hexagonal bead

Ending

9 each

4 5 6 7 7 7

Beginning

Ending

Beginning
wire 70cm(28″)

Pass wire to
front and
to back
alternately to make miniature
three-dimensional.

Designs photographes on page 46.
①④⑦⑧⑮ EARRINGS

Glue small beads on an earring
with a circular metal base 2.8cm(1 1/8″).

⑤ RINGS

Decide length of ring
wire according to size
of your finger.

wire 60cm(24″)

Beginning

Ending

2 wires 40cm(16″)

Ending

Attach another
wire 40cm(16″)
long.

Ending

000
0000   4
5
7

7

7
4

Beginning

2 wires 40cm(16″)
wire 20cm(8″)

wire 60cm(24″)

Ending   Beginning

2 wires 40cm(16″)
wire 20cm(8″)

Attach another
wire 40cm(16″)
long.

Ending

Ending

Beginning

Attach another wire
20cm(8″) long.

Ending

9
8
7
0
4

Attach another
wire 40cm(16″)
long.

Beginning

Attach another
wire 40cm(16″) long.

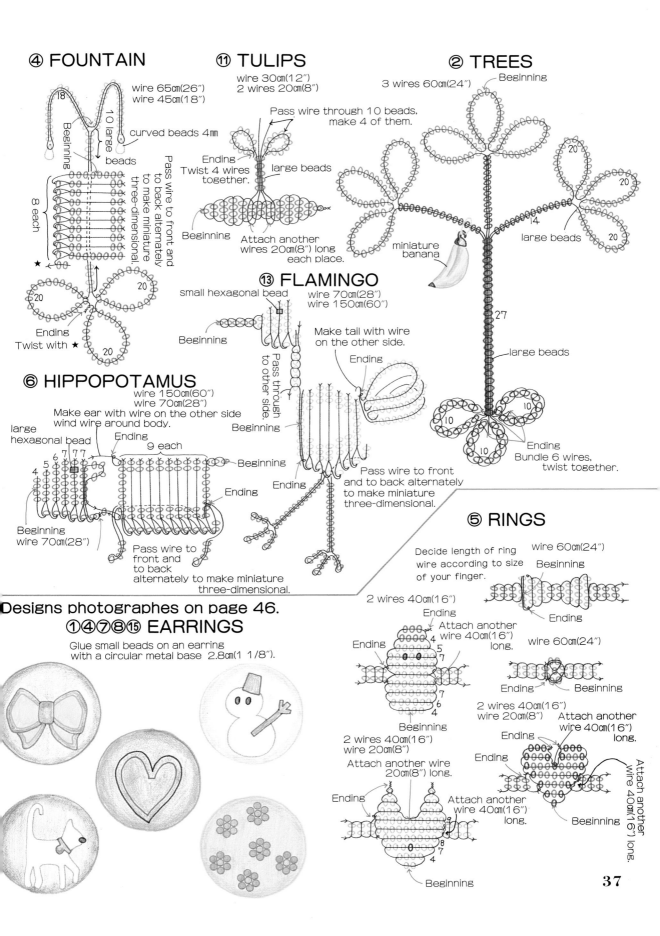

37

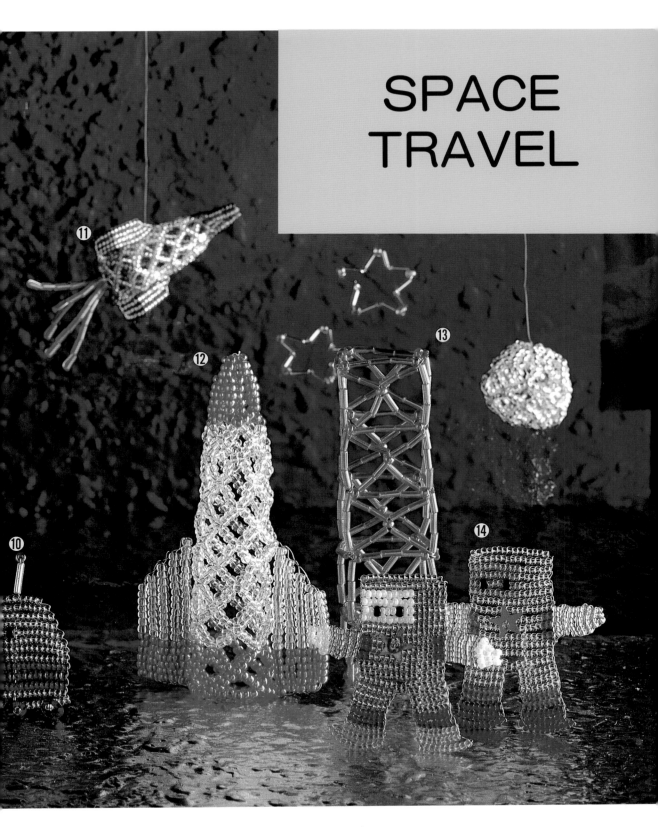

SPACE TRAVEL

Designs ①-⑭   Use large beads unless otherwise indicated.
Materials : small circular beads, large circular beads, bugle beads (6mm) (9mm),
small star-shaped spangle, large star-shaped spangle, circular spangle,
31ga wire,

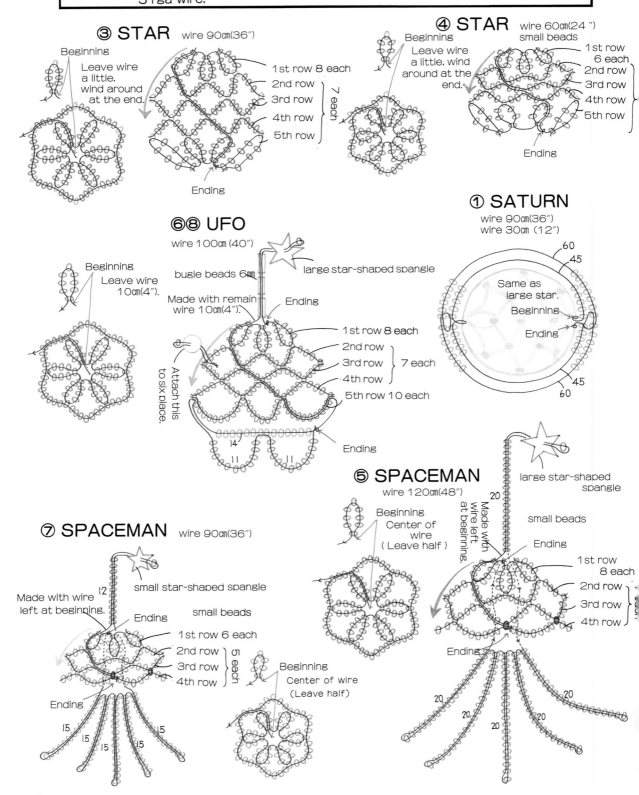

③ STAR   wire 90cm(36")

Beginning
Leave wire a little, wind around at the end.

1st row 8 each
2nd row
3rd row   7 each
4th row
5th row

Ending

④ STAR   wire 60cm(24")   small beads

Beginning
Leave wire a little, wind around at the end.

1st row 6 each
2nd row
3rd row
4th row
5th row

Ending

① SATURN
wire 90cm(36")
wire 30cm (12")

60
45
Same as large star.
Beginning
Ending
45
60

⑥⑧ UFO
wire 100cm (40")

bugle beads 6mm
large star-shaped spangle

Made with remain wire 10cm(4").
Ending

Beginning
Leave wire 10cm(4").

Attach this to six place.

1st row 8 each
2nd row
3rd row   7 each
4th row
5th row 10 each

14
11   11
Ending

⑤ SPACEMAN
wire 120cm(48")

large star-shaped spangle
small beads

20

Made with wire left at beginning.

Beginning
Center of wire
(Leave half)

Ending

1st row 8 each
2nd row
3rd row
4th row

Ending

20
20   20
20

⑦ SPACEMAN   wire 90cm(36")

small star-shaped spangle
small beads

Made with wire left at beginning.

12

Ending

1st row 6 each
2nd row
3rd row   5 each
4th row

Ending

Beginning
Center of wire
(Leave half)

15   15
15   15
15

40

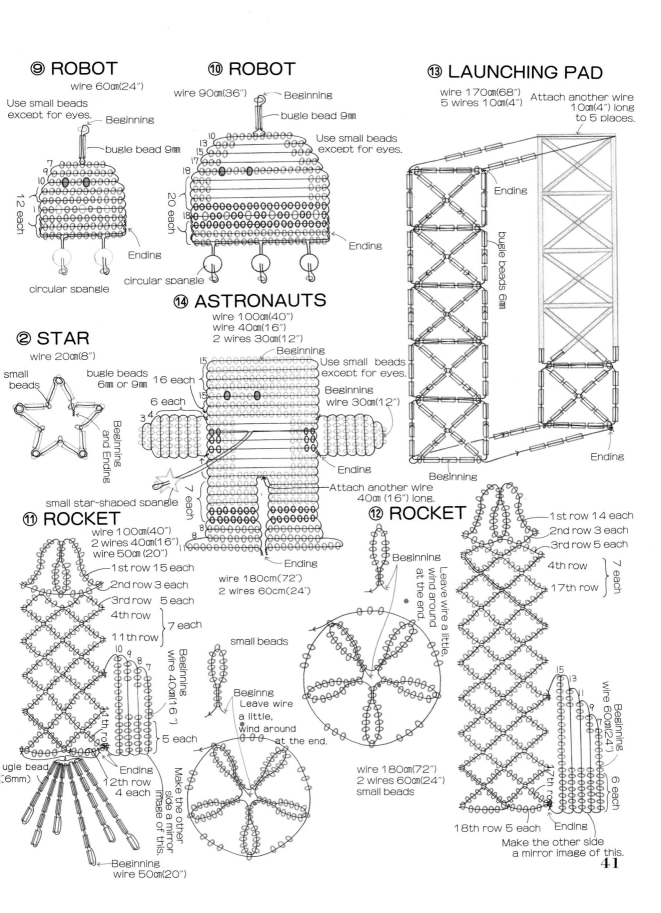

⑨ ROBOT

wire 60cm(24")

Use small beads
except for eyes.

Beginning

bugle bead 9mm

7
9
10
12 each

Ending

circular spangle

⑩ ROBOT

wire 90cm(36")

Beginning

bugle bead 9mm

Use small beads
except for eyes.

10
13
15
17
18
20 each
18

Ending

circular spangle

⑬ LAUNCHING PAD

wire 170cm(68")
5 wires 10cm(4")

Attach another wire
10cm(4") long
to 5 places.

Ending

bugle beads 6mm

Beginning

Ending

② STAR

wire 20cm(8")

small beads

bugle beads
6mm or 9mm

Beginning
and Ending

small star-shaped spangle

⑭ ASTRONAUTS

wire 100cm(40")
wire 40cm(16")
2 wires 30cm(12")

Beginning

Use small beads
except for eyes.

Beginning
wire 30cm(12")

15
16 each
15
6 each
3 4
7 each
11

Ending

Attach another wire
40cm (16") long.

Ending

wire 180cm(72")
2 wires 60cm(24")

⑪ ROCKET

wire 100cm(40")
2 wires 40cm(16")
wire 50cm(20")

1st row 15 each
2nd row 3 each
3rd row 5 each
4th row
11th row } 7 each

10 9 8 7

Beginning
wire 40cm(16")

5 each

11th row

bugle bead
(6mm)

Ending
12th row
4 each

Make the other
side a mirror
image of this.

Beginning
wire 50cm(20")

⑫ ROCKET

small beads

Beginning
Leave wire a little,
wind around
at the end.

Beginnng
Leave wire
a little,
wind around
at the end.

wire 180cm(72")
2 wires 60cm(24")
small beads

1st row 14 each
2nd row 3 each
3rd row 5 each
4th row
17th row } 7 each

15
13
11
7 each
6 each

Beginning
wire 60cm(24")

17th row

18th row 5 each

Ending

Make the other side
a mirror image of this.

41

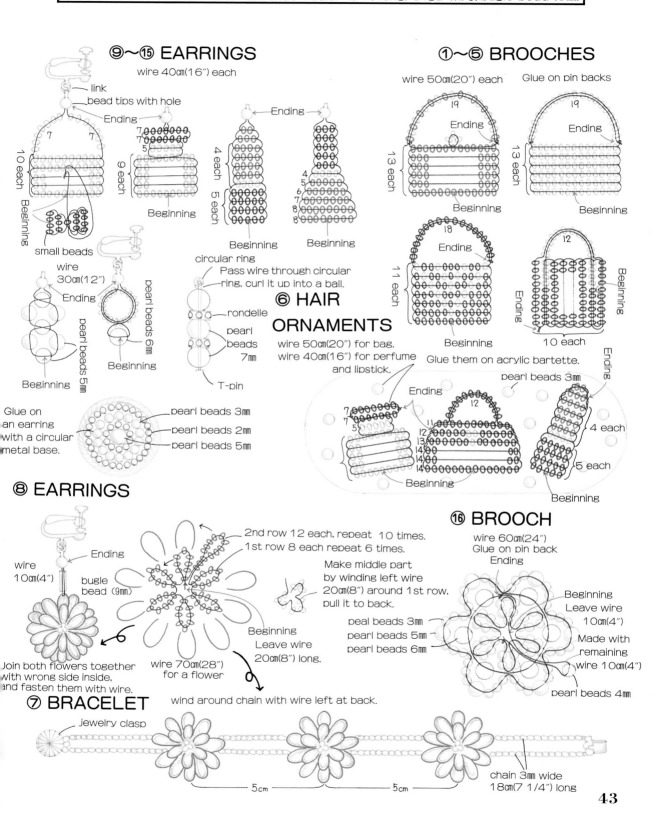

Designs ①-⑯   Use large beads unless otherwise indicated.
Materials : small circular beads, large cirular beads, pearl beads (2mm) (2.5mm) (3mm)
(4mm) (5mm) (6mm) (7mm),bead tip with hole, circular ring, rondelles earring clips, barrette,
pin back, jewelry clasp, chain 3mm wide 18cm(7 1/4") long, 31ga wire, bugle bead (9mm)

⑨~⑮ EARRINGS

wire 40cm(16") each

link
bead tips with hole
Ending

7   7
10 each
Beginning

small beads

wire 30cm(12")
Ending
pearl beads 6mm
Beginning
pearl beads 5mm
Beginning

7
7
5
9 each
Beginning

4 each
5 each
4
5
6
7
8
8
Ending
Beginning
Beginning

pearl beads 7mm

circular ring
Pass wire through circular ring, curl it up into a ball.

⑥ HAIR ORNAMENTS

rondelle
pearl beads 7mm
T-pin

wire 50cm(20") for bag.
wire 40cm(16") for perfume and lipstick.

Glue on an earring with a circular metal base.

pearl beads 3mm
pearl beads 2mm
pearl beads 5mm

① ~ ⑤ BROOCHES

wire 50cm(20") each   Glue on pin backs

19   19
Ending   Ending
13 each   13 each
Beginning   Beginning

18
Ending
11 each
Beginning

12
Beginning
Ending
10 each

Ending
7
7
5
11
12
13
14
14
14
Beginning

12
Glue them on acrylic bartette.
pearl beads 3mm
4 each
5 each
Beginning
Ending

⑧ EARRINGS

wire 10cm(4")
Ending
bugle bead (9mm)

Join both flowers together with wrong side inside, and fasten them with wire.

2nd row 12 each, repeat 10 times.
1st row 8 each repeat 6 times.

Make middle part by winding left wire 20cm(8") around 1st row, pull it to back.

peal beads 3mm
pearl beads 5mm
pearl beads 6mm

Beginning
Leave wire 20cm(8") long.

wire 70cm(28") for a flower

⑯ BROOCH

wire 60cm(24")
Glue on pin back
Ending

Beginning
Leave wire 10cm(4")

Made with remaining wire 10cm(4")

pearl beads 4mm

⑦ BRACELET

wind around chain with wire left at back.

jewelry clasp

5cm   5cm

chain 3mm wide 18cm(7 1/4") long

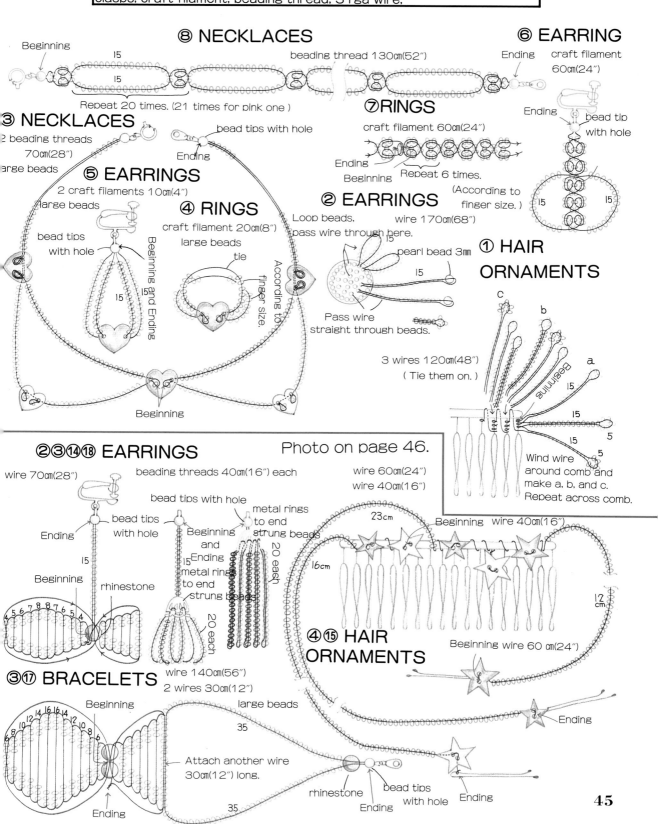

Designs ①-⑧   Use small beads unless otherwise indicated.
Materials : small circular beads, large circular beads, pearl beads (3mm),
bead tip with hole, parts of earring, comb, heart-shaped acrylic-mirror,
clasps, craft filament, beading thread, 31ga wire,

⑧ NECKLACES

Beginning
15
15
beading thread 130cm(52")
Repeat 20 times. (21 times for pink one)

⑥ EARRING
Ending   craft filament
60cm(24")
Ending   bead tip
with hole
15   15

③ NECKLACES
2 beading threads
70cm(28")
large beads
bead tips with hole
Ending

⑦ RINGS
craft filament 60cm(24")
Ending
Beginning   Repeat 6 times.
(According to
finger size.)

⑤ EARRINGS
2 craft filaments 10cm(4")
large beads
bead tips
with hole
15   15

④ RINGS
craft filament 20cm(8")
large beads
tie
According to finger size.
Beginning and Ending

② EARRINGS
Loop beads,
pass wire through here.
wire 170cm(68")
15
pearl bead 3mm
15
Pass wire
straight through beads.

① HAIR
ORNAMENTS
c
b
a
Beginning
15
15
15
5
5
Wind wire
around comb and
make a, b, and c.
Repeat across comb.

Beginning

②③⑭⑱ EARRINGS   Photo on page 46.

wire 70cm(28")
Ending
15
Beginning
rhinestone

beading threads 40cm(16") each
bead tips with hole
bead tips
with hole
Beginning
and
Ending
metal rings
to end
strung beads
15
metal rings
to end
strung beads
20 each
20 each

metal rings
to end
strung beads
20 each

wire 60cm(24")
wire 40cm(16")

④⑮ HAIR
ORNAMENTS
23cm
16cm
Beginning wire 40cm(16")
12cm
Beginning wire 60 cm(24")
Ending

③⑰ BRACELETS
wire 140cm(56")
2 wires 30cm(12")
Beginning   large beads
14 16 16 14
12   12
10   10
8   8
6   6
4 5 6 7 8 8 7 6 5 4
35
Attach another wire
30cm(12") long.
35
rhinestone
Ending
bead tips
with hole
Ending
Ending
Ending

45

FASHION STATEMENTS

46

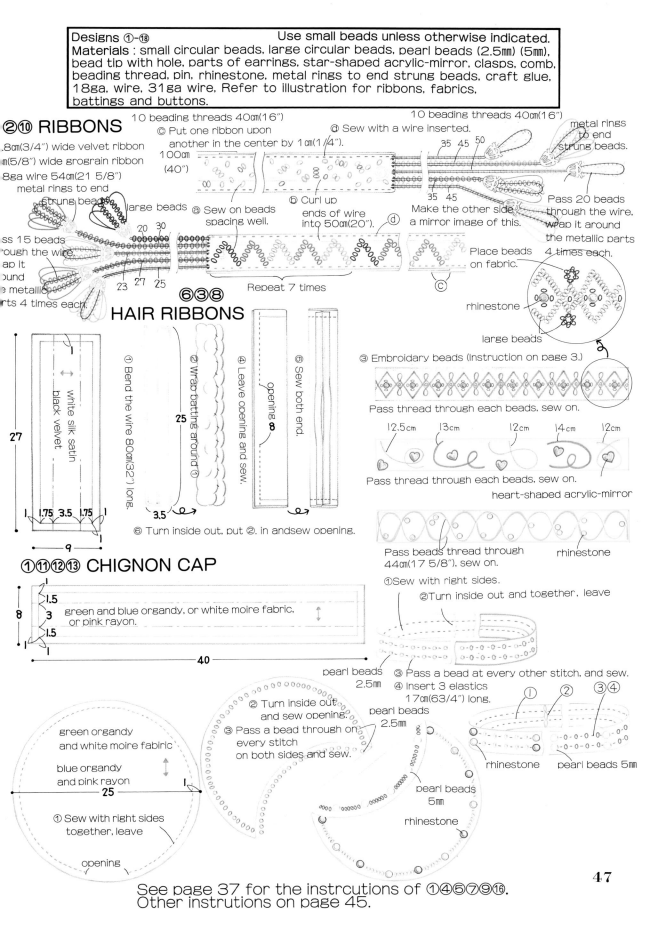

Designs ①-⑱   Use small beads unless otherwise indicated.
Materials : small circular beads, large circular beads, pearl beads (2.5mm) (5mm),
bead tip with hole, parts of earrings, star-shaped acrylic-mirror, clasps, comb,
beading thread, pin, rhinestone, metal rings to end strung beads, craft glue,
18ga, wire, 31ga wire, Refer to illustration for ribbons, fabrics,
battings and buttons.

②⑩ RIBBONS

.8cm(3/4") wide velvet ribbon
m(5/8") wide grograin ribbon
8ga wire 54cm(21 5/8")
    metal rings to end
    strung beads.

large beads

20 30
23 27 25

10 beading threads 40cm(16")
© Put one ribbon upon
another in the center by 1cm(1/4").
100cm
(40")

ⓐ Sew on beads
spacing well.

ⓑ Curl up
ends of wire
into 50cm(20").

Repeat 7 times

ⓓ Sew with a wire inserted.
35 45 50

35 45

Make the other side
a mirror image of this.

ⓒ

10 beading threads 40cm(16")

metal rings
to end
strung beads.

Pass 20 beads
through the wire,
wrap it around
the metallic parts
4 times each.

ss 15 beads
rough the wire.
ap it
ound
e metallic
arts 4 times each.

Place beads
on fabric.

rhinestone

large beads

③ Embroidary beads (Instruction on page 3.)

Pass thread through each beads, sew on.

12.5cm   13cm   12cm   14cm   12cm

Pass thread through each beads, sew on.

heart-shaped acrylic-mirror

rhinestone

Pass beads thread through
44cm(17 5/8"), sew on.

①Sew with right sides.
②Turn inside out and together, leave

③ Pass a bead at every other stitch, and sew.
④ Insert 3 elastics
    17cm(63/4") long.

① ② ③④

rhinestone   pearl beads 5mm

⑥③⑧ HAIR RIBBONS

white silk satin
black velvet

27

1.75 3.5 1.75

9

① Bend the wire 80cm(32") long.

② Wrap batting around ①

25

3.5

④ Leave opening and sew.

opening
8

⑤ Sew both end.

⑥ Turn inside out, put ②. in andsew opening.

①⑪⑫⑬ CHIGNON CAP

1.5
3
1.5
8

green and blue organdy, or white moire fabric,
or pink rayon.

40

pearl beads
2.5mm

② Turn inside out
and sew opening.

③ Pass a bead through on
every stitch
on both sides and sew.

pearl beads
2.5mm

green organdy
and white moire fabiric

blue organdy
and pink rayon
25

① Sew with right sides
together, leave

opening

pearl beads
5mm

rhinestone

See page 37 for the instrcutions of ①④⑤⑦⑨⑯.
Other instrutions on page 45.

Designs ①-⑫   Use large beads unless otherwise indicated.
Materials : small circular beads, large circular beads, oval pearl beads (3×6mm),
curved beads (3mm), small spangle, large spangle, 31ga wire.

① ARIES Mar.21--Apr.19

wire 80cm(32")
2 wires 20cm(8")

Ending

Attach another
wire 15cm(6)long.

Attach another
wire 20cm(8") long,
each place.

Beginning

Ending

② TAURUS Apr.20--May.20

wire 60cm(24")
2 wires 20cm(8")
wire 15cm(6")

Ending

Ending

12
12
11
11
10
9

Attach another
wire 20cm(8") long,
each place.

Beginning

③ GEMINI
May.21--Jun.21

wire 60cm(24")

Ending

small bead
small star-shaped
spangle

9
10
12
14
15
16
15

8

Beginning

④ CANCER
Jun.22--Jul.22

wire 80cm(32")

curved beads 3mm

Ending

Beginning

⑤ LEO
Jul.23--Aug.22

wire 80cm(32")
2 wires 20cm(8")

Ending

Attach
another wire
20cm(8") long,
each place.

Beginning

Ending

⑥ VIRGO
Aug.23--Sep.22

wire 60cm(24")
2 wires 20cm(8")

Ending

Beginning
wire 20cm

Ending

Beginning

⑦ LIBRA Sep.23--Oct.23

wire 110cm(44")
wire 70cm(28")

20
16
curved bead 4mm
small beads
Attach
another wire
70cm(28") long

10   10
10
9
8
7

Ending

Beginning

⑧ SCORPIO Oct.24--Nov.22

wire 100cm(40")
curved beads 3mm

Beginning

Ending

Ending

⑨ SAGITTARIUS
Nov.23--Dec.21

wire 80cm(32")

oval pearl beads
3×6mm

13

9   7   6

Ending

Beginning

⑩ CAPRICORN
Dec.22--Jan.19

Ending

Attach
another wire
15cm(6") long

wire 60cm(24")
2 wires 20cm(8")
wire 15cm(6")

small star-shaped
spangles

9
11
11
10
9
7   6
5
4   3
2

Beginning

Attach
another wire
20cm (8") long,
each place.

⑪ AQUARIUS
Jan.20--Feb.18

wire 80cm(32")

small beads

13
11
9

12
13

17

14
13
12
10

Beginning

Ending

⑫ PISCES
Feb.19--Mar.20

wire 70cm(28")
wire 20cm(8") Beginning

10 9
8   10 9   5 3 4 5
6   4

Beginning

Ending

Ending

48